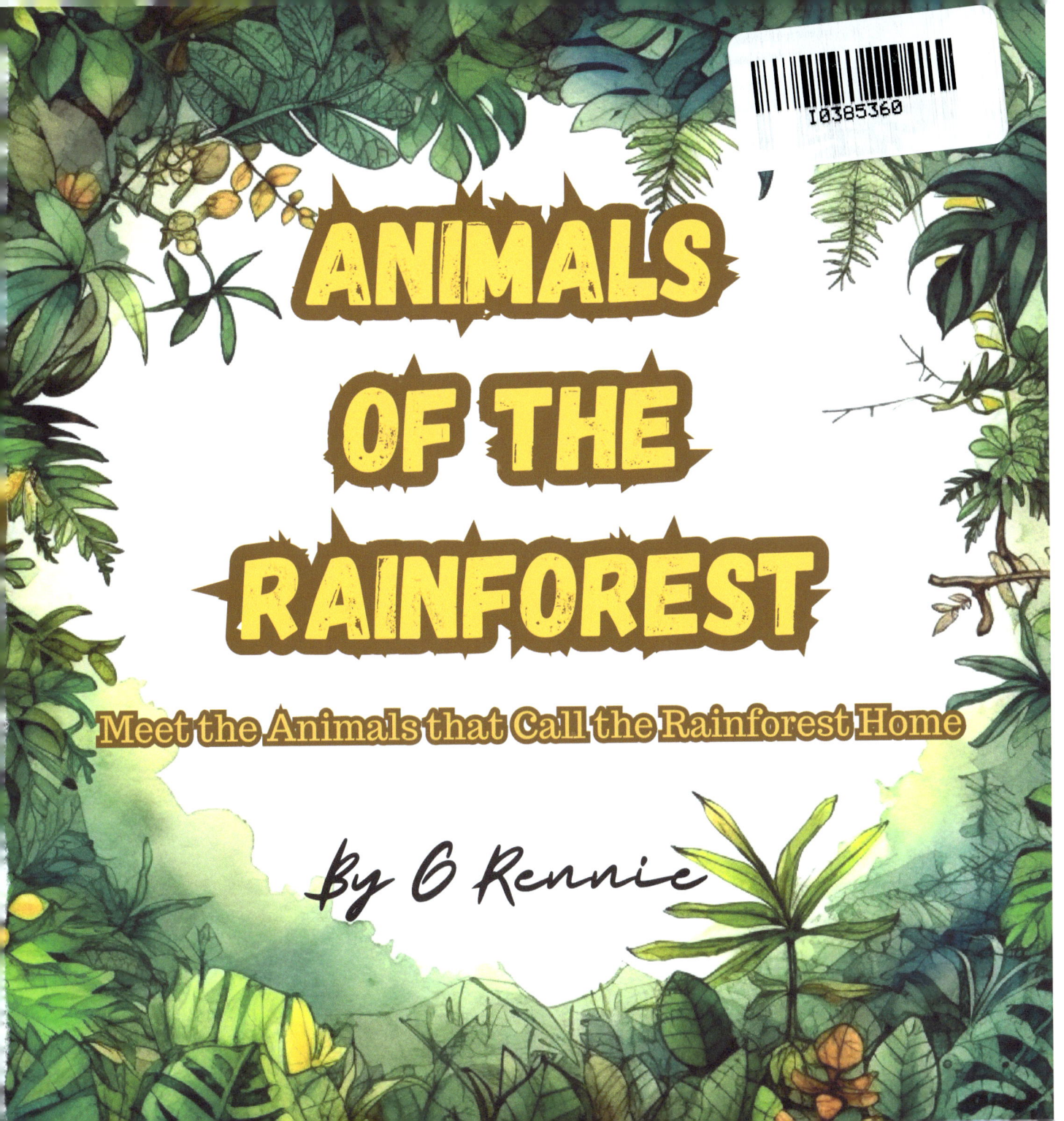

Contents

Black Caiman	4
Sloth	6
Macaw	8
Jaguar	10
Capybara	12
Anaconda	14
Toucan	16
Poison Dart Frog	18
Armadillo	20
Squirrel Monkey	22
River Dolphin	24

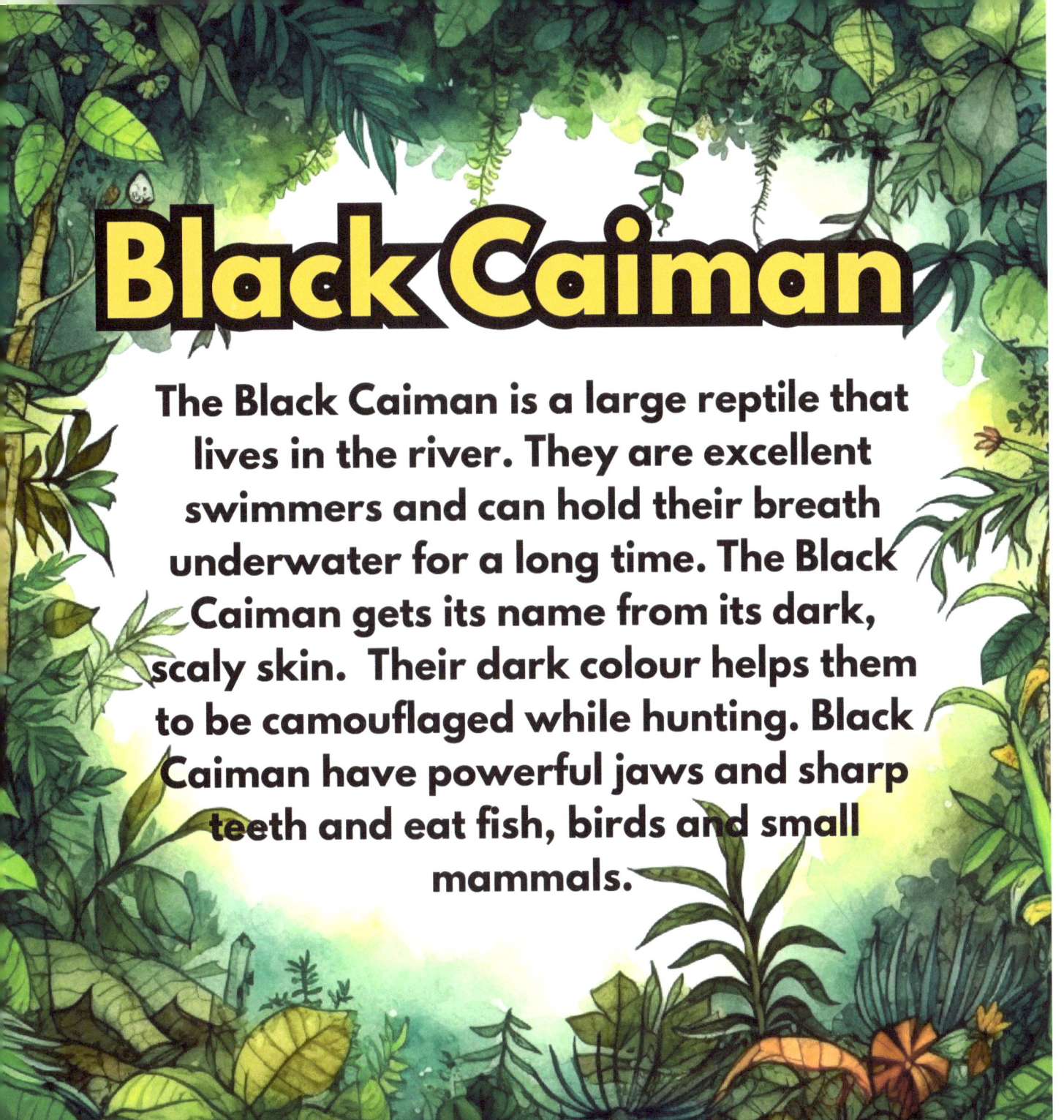

Black Caiman

The Black Caiman is a large reptile that lives in the river. They are excellent swimmers and can hold their breath underwater for a long time. The Black Caiman gets its name from its dark, scaly skin. Their dark colour helps them to be camouflaged while hunting. Black Caiman have powerful jaws and sharp teeth and eat fish, birds and small mammals.

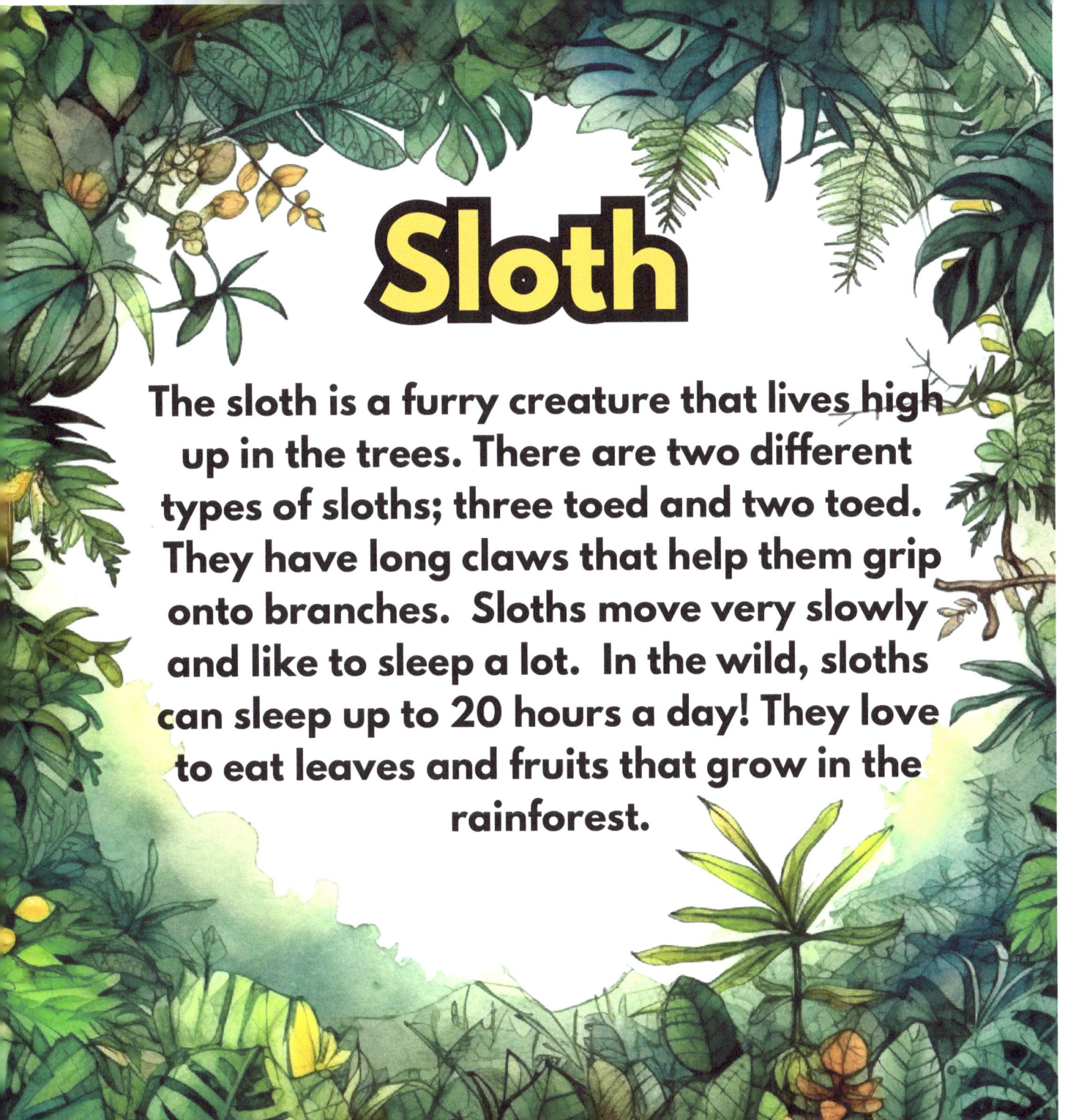

Sloth

The sloth is a furry creature that lives high up in the trees. There are two different types of sloths; three toed and two toed. They have long claws that help them grip onto branches. Sloths move very slowly and like to sleep a lot. In the wild, sloths can sleep up to 20 hours a day! They love to eat leaves and fruits that grow in the rainforest.

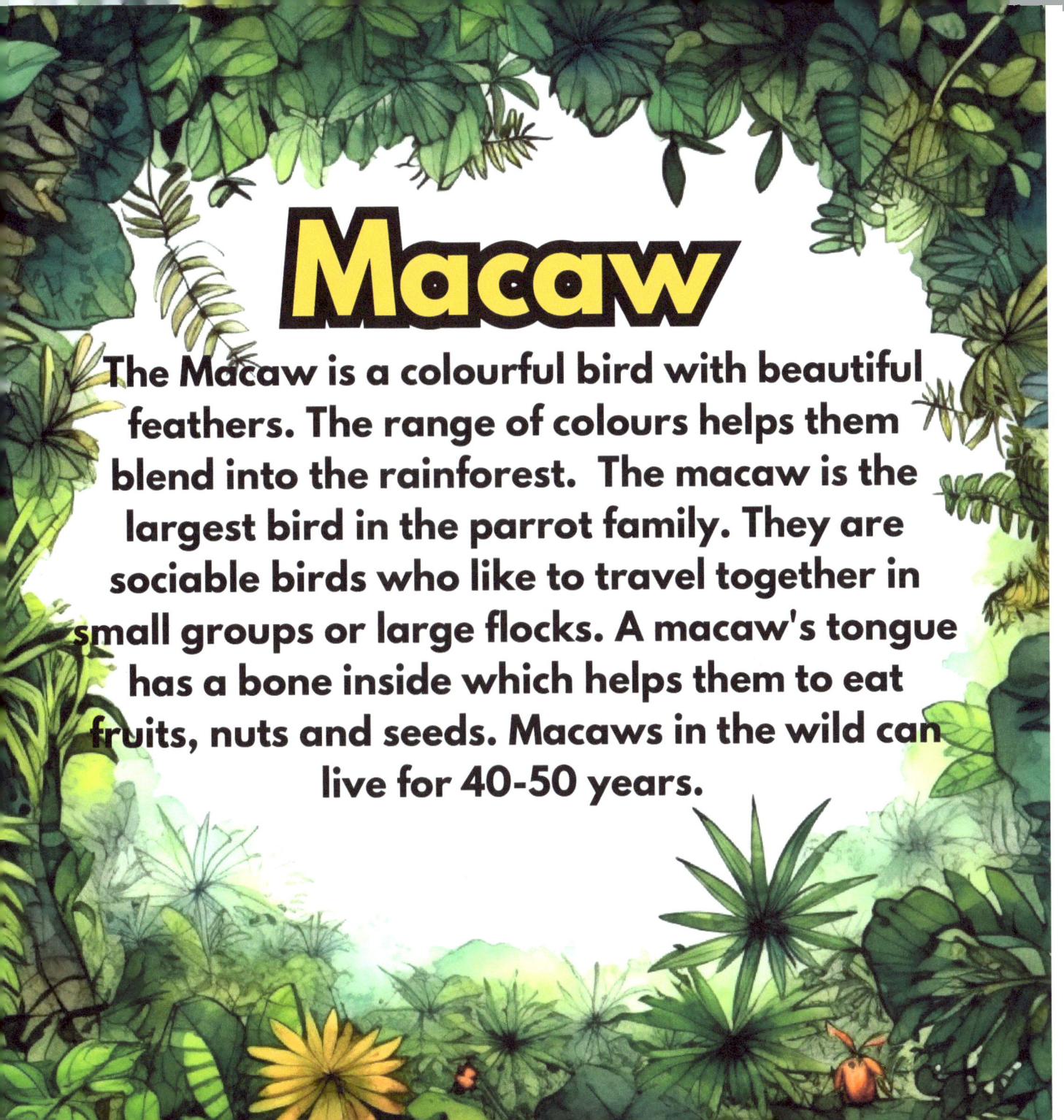

Macaw

The Macaw is a colourful bird with beautiful feathers. The range of colours helps them blend into the rainforest. The macaw is the largest bird in the parrot family. They are sociable birds who like to travel together in small groups or large flocks. A macaw's tongue has a bone inside which helps them to eat fruits, nuts and seeds. Macaws in the wild can live for 40-50 years.

Jaguar

The Jaguar is a big cat with their coats covered in beautiful, dark spots. Jaguars can be mistaken for leopards as they have similar markings. Unlike many cats, Jaguars do not avoid water and are excellent, strong swimmers. They are also skilled climbers and hunters too. Jaguars have strong jaws and teeth and will eat almost any animals they find in the wild.

Capybara

The Capybara are semi-aquatic animals that can live happily on land or on riverbanks. They love to be in the water and swim. Capybaras are social animals who often gather in groups to stay safe from predators. These groups can range from 10 - 100 capybaras at a time. The capybara has special scent glands on their bottoms that they use to communicate with each other.

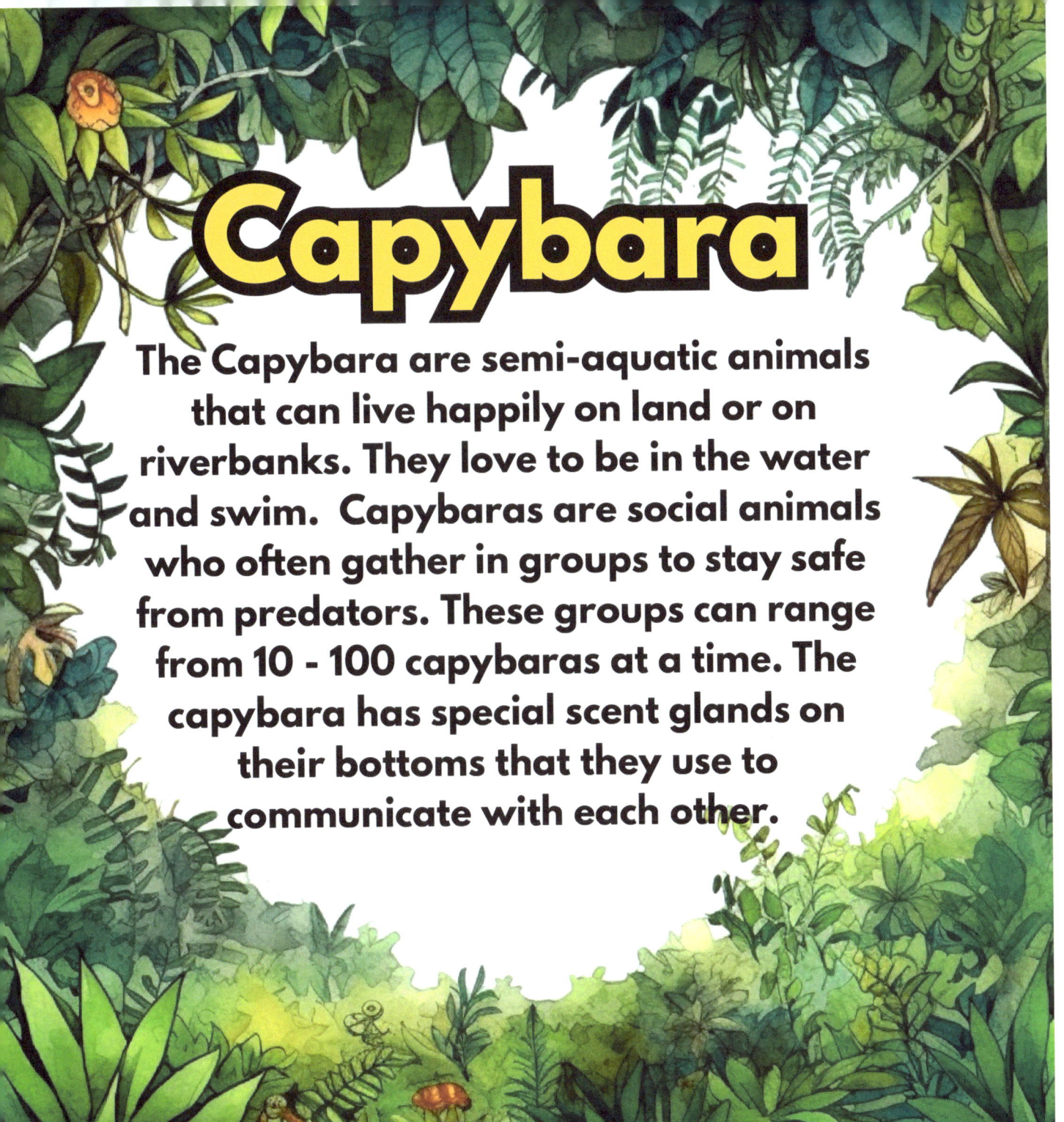

Anaconda

Green anacondas are one of the largest known snakes in the world. Female anacondas are much larger than the males. They are very long and powerful but are not venomous. Anacondas like to spend a lot of time in the water and are excellent swimmers. They are sometimes known as water boas. Anacondas squeeze their prey tightly and eat animals like fish, birds, and even small deer. In the wild, anacondas can live for about 10 years.

Toucan

The toucan is a bird with a big, colourful beak. Male toucans have a larger beak than females. Toucans use their large beaks and long tongues to reach fruits up in the trees but they are omnivores and also eat insects and lizards. Despite having large beaks, toucans have small wings so need to flap their wings a lot to fly. In the wild, toucans can live up to 20 years.

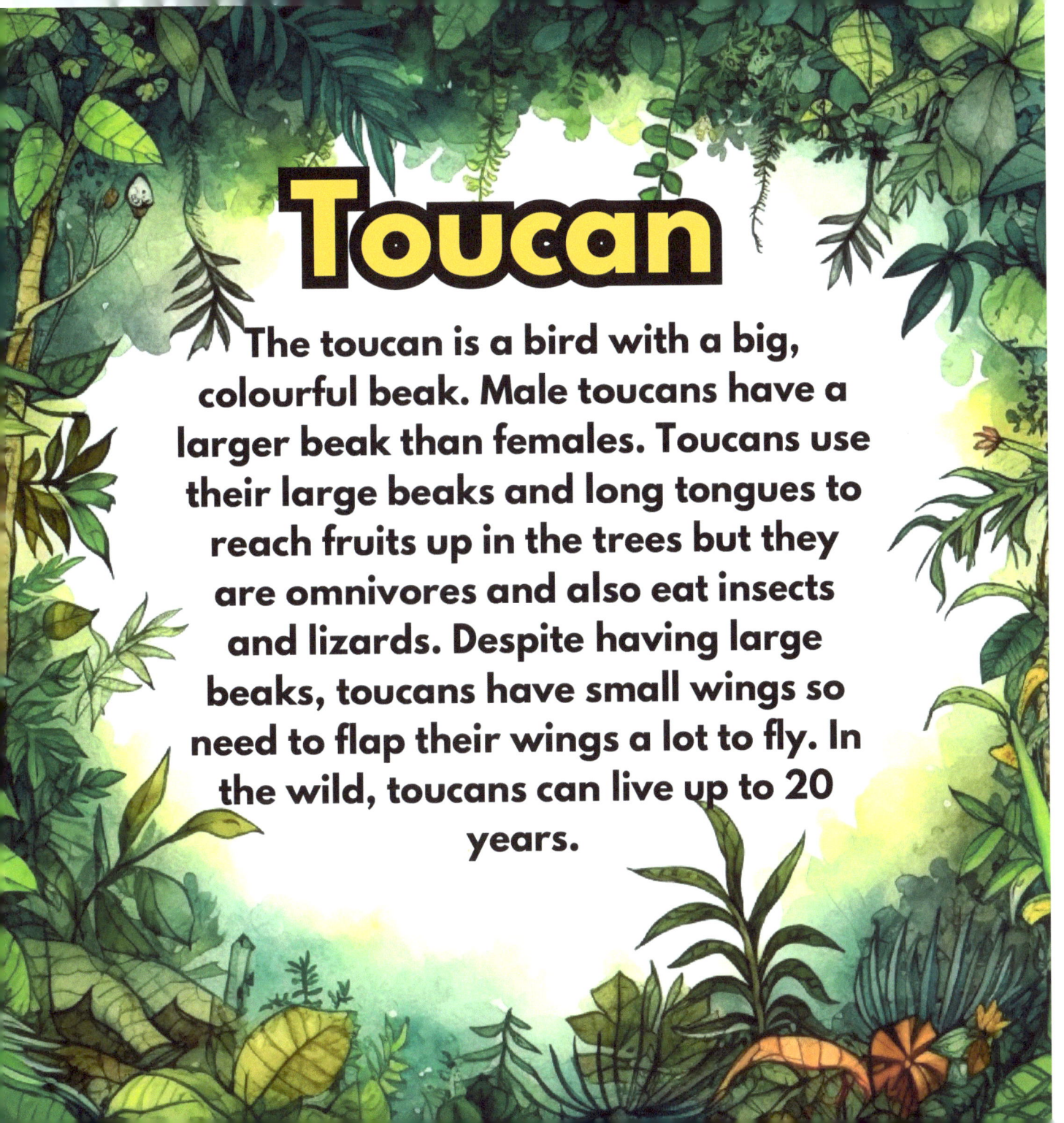

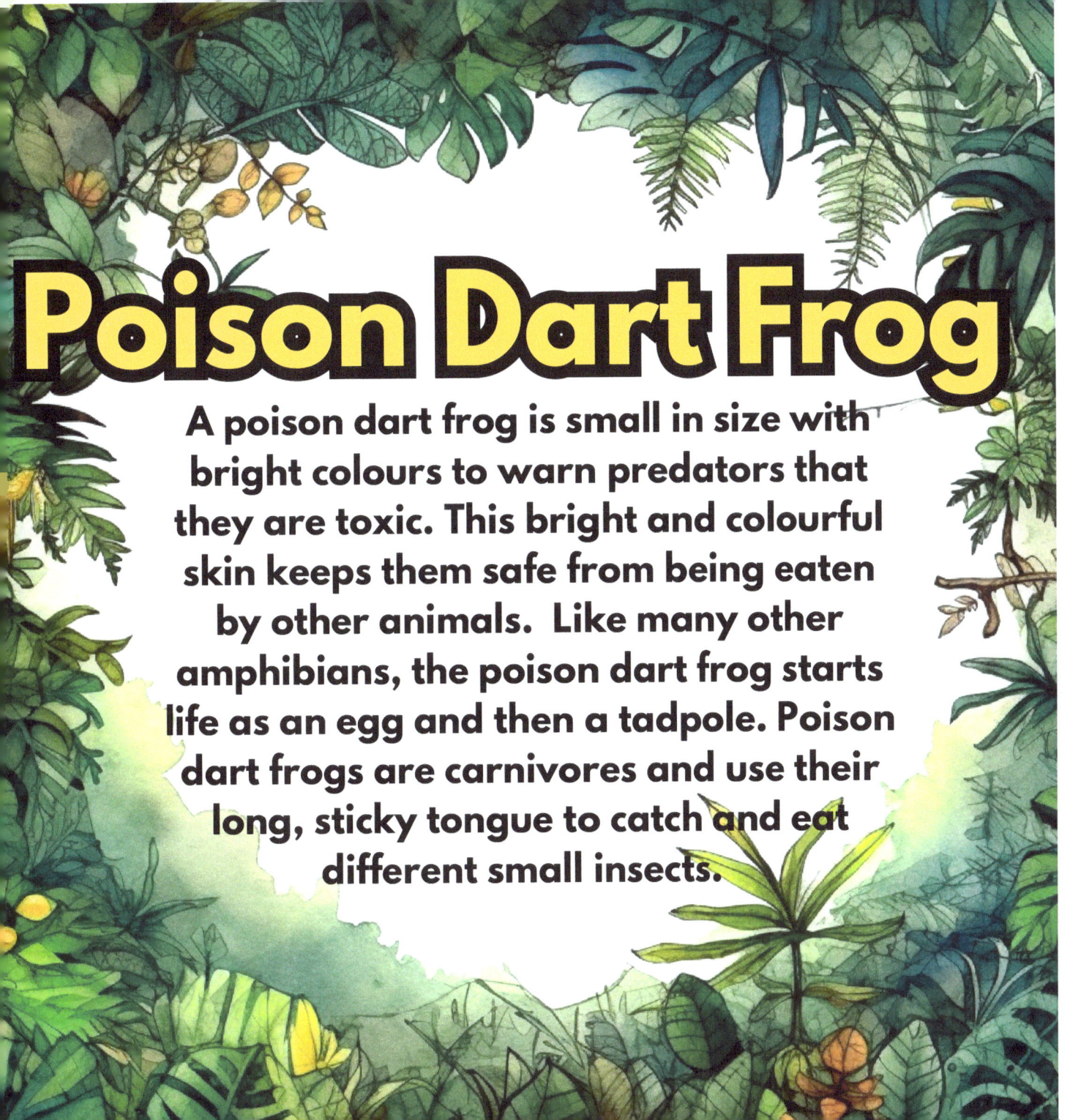

Poison Dart Frog

A poison dart frog is small in size with bright colours to warn predators that they are toxic. This bright and colourful skin keeps them safe from being eaten by other animals. Like many other amphibians, the poison dart frog starts life as an egg and then a tadpole. Poison dart frogs are carnivores and use their long, sticky tongue to catch and eat different small insects.

Armadillo

The giant armadillo is a unique animal with hard shell-like skin. They use their long front claws to search for insects and fruits to eat. Their claws also help them to be expert diggers. The giant armadillo can have between 80 - 100 teeth! When threatened, armadillos curl up in to a ball to protect themselves.

Squirrel Monkey

The Squirrel Monkey is a small and playful monkey. They love to spend most of their time in trees, jumping between the branches. They use their tails to balance as they move from tree to tree. Squirrel monkeys live in groups called troops and take care of each other. They are omnivores who mainly eat fruits and insects.

River Dolphin

The river dolphin is a special kind of dolphin that lives in the Amazon River. It is sometimes known as the pink river dolphin because, unlike the ocean dolphin, it has a pale pink body. River dolphins are very good swimmers and can swim backwards as well as forwards. They use sound to find fish and other animals in the river to eat.

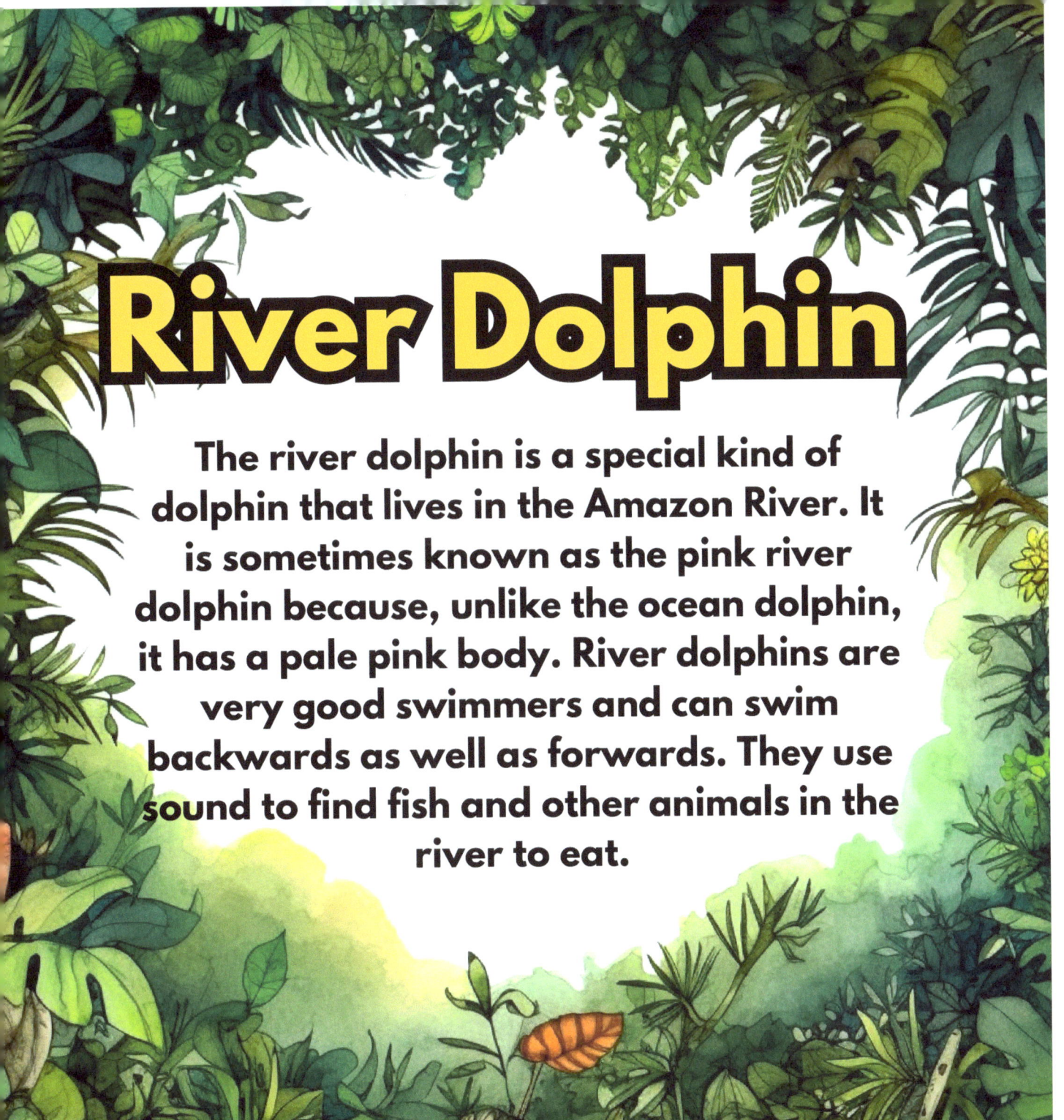

Puma

The Puma is a strong and powerful big cat. Pumas can also be known as a mountain lion. They are excellent at jumping and climbing trees and can even swim if they have to! Pumas are carnivores and in the tropical Amazon rainforest pumas prey on smaller animals including monkeys and capybaras. Pumas are nocturnal, solitary animals but can communicate with each other through growls and whistles.

www.ingramcontent.com/pod-product-compliance
Lightning Source LLC
Chambersburg PA
CBHW040022130526
44590CB00036B/65